How to be Witty: The Ultimate Guide to Becoming More Clever, Charming, and Engaging with People

By: Clayton Geoffreys

Table of Contents

Foreword

Have you ever wondered why certain people are so funny? Or even how some people just have a way with words that makes people smile? I know I have. I spent my early twenties wondering why it was that some people were just so witty. What is it about wit that makes people love it? Where does it come from? Most importantly, can a person become wittier? These are all questions that I set out to explore, and in this book, I answer these questions. This book is a concise summary of all the findings that I've pulled together from my time researching the subject. Hopefully from reading *How to be Witty: The Ultimate Guide to Becoming More Clever, Charming, and Engaging with People*, I can pass along some of the abundance of information I have learned about why wit plays such a big role in our lives and how to make it part of yours. Thank you for downloading my book. Hope you enjoy and if you do, please do not forget to leave a review!

Also, check out my website at claytongeoffreys.com to join my exclusive list where I let you know about my latest books. To thank you for your purchase, you can also go to my site to download a free book!

Cheers,

Clayton Geoffreys

Why is Being Witty Important?

Everybody wants to be a comedian nowadays. Men want to be "that guy", the one who slays male competitors with witty repartee and absconds with admiring girls. Even some women aspire to be the funny girl who keeps her man in stitches. It is no doubt that riotously humorous people are the life of the party, and their witty wordplay is sorely coveted by less funny folks. However, popular perception aside, just how important is it for one to be witty? Psychologists, sociologists and others have turned their spotlights on this human ability with the intent of answering just this question. Their answer is not surprising. The ability to be humorous correlates to increased personal well-being, social interaction and health. Nature favors funny people, and funny people benefit immensely from this one, personal trait.

Witty people gain social chops just by virtue of being funny.[1] Few people fail to enjoy time spent laughing with good company. However, natural wit bestows upon one more than the mere ability to evoke laughter. Persons who possess wit and a healthy dose of intuition are able to gauge the moods of their audience by measuring the reception of their various jokes, barbs and tall tales.[1] Armed with this perception, the witty guy or gal can purposefully alienate or endear others by directing the tone of their humor.[1] Masterfully funny people can employ wit in ways that cause others to flit to them and like them. Specifically, one's wit is used as a tool to expose and identify others in the environment that shares similar dispositions and propensities.[2] In romantic scenarios, fine-tuned wit can equate to "getting" the girl or guy. In fact, various studies show that male wit or humor often sparks romantic interest in the female kind. Conversely female wit is that which sustains burgeoning relationships for the long haul.[2] Humor is so important in intimate relationships that its presence is linked to marital satisfaction in all cultures.[1]

Wit is not merely beneficial to one's love life and social standing. The ability to exercise wit and generally appreciate humor is a prime factor in fostering mental health. Persons with high degrees of wit and mirth tend to enjoy a high degree of consistency between what they perceive to be their ideal selves and what they believe to be their actual self. They tend to enjoy an increased sense of self-esteem throughout the duration of their lives, and this equates to a life filled with rewarding social interactions. Consequently, witty persons are relatively immune from negative self-perception, and they generally evade the specter of mental illnesses such as depression.[3] Psychologists are acutely aware of these correlations, and they use the ability to appreciate jokes and exhibit wit as a marker of mental illness or lack thereof. Poor assessment of wit or humor in a person are even perceived by some doctors to indicate deficits in brain function or neurological problems.[2]

Finally, humor and wit also equate to health benefits that extend beyond the brain and central nervous system. Humor and wit generally elevate one's spirits. However, persons who possess the specific ability to laugh in the face of their own life stressors are able to distance themselves from them. Subsequently, tension associated with stress either abates in the sufferer or fails to develop at all. Lack of tension leads to a drop in or non-production of perilous stress hormones that might otherwise overwhelm the bodies of less humorous persons.[2] This decrease in stress hormones then promotes health, because it protects important organic systems like the cardiovascular system and the endocrine system. Humor is known to boost immunity to disease and infection, as well. Thus, those propounding laughter as the best medicine are right.

7 Reasons Why Being Witty Can Elevate Conversation Skills

People who master witticism can look forward to a lifetime of lively conversations. Insertion of appropriate humor into any conversation not only accords temporary enjoyment to the involved parties; it has many benefits that extend well past the point when the laughter stops. Detailed below are 7 of the benefits associated with the use of wit in day-to-day conversation.

1. Wit is Appreciated

The funny guy makes a real contribution to any conversation in which he partakes.[3] This stems from the fact that wit is valued at some level by every society on Earth. Unfortunately, most societies have evolved in such a way that individuals have become fearful of perpetrating personal acts of humor. This fear is witnessed every day in modern society. All societies have deep-rooted, taboo topics that defy humorous commentary. However, today's comedic landscape is particularly fraught with difficulties that deter persons from joking about virtually anything. Everyone feels safe in their assurance that Holocaust or 9/11 jokes are wrong. That goes without saying. Still, the advent of political correctness has introduced ever expanding grey areas of what is and is not permissible to be funny. Go-to Polish jokes and dumb blonde jokes that were a comedic staple for generations are now deemed ethnic slurs and acts of misogyny. Modern audiences perceive race based jokes and overtly sexual jokes as hateful and crass. Since many peoples' repertoire of wit is limited, they believe that wit is best relegated to professional comedians who know how to safely navigate this new and improved reality.[2] As a result, truly witty individuals who arrive on scene with jokes in-hand—

jokes that are appreciated by all—are perceived to be gifted and daring mavericks who excel at a dying art.

2. Wit Provokes Laughter

Much like yawning, no one can withstand the sight or sound of another's laughter without succumbing to the impulse himself. Further, laughter promotes more than a transitory, elevated mood. As stated earlier, laughter promotes myriad health benefits, and it has the added advantage of endearing persons to the source of all this laughter, the witty person themselves. Consequently, witty people are sought after because the benefits of being in their company are immense.[4]

3. Shared Wit Solidifies Relationships

Laughter is contagious. However, laughter is not sustained unless the witty person and his audience generally share a similar sense of humor. Further, what persons find humorous typically resonates with immediate life circumstances, general outlook on life and innate propensities concerning what is and is not perceived to be funny. Consequently, exploitation of wit allows persons to identify who in the immediate environment would make a suitable match for dating, friendship or work compatibility. Similarly, bystanders who partake in the fun are equally able to assess who is in their own "in-group" by observing other people who laugh at the same jokes.

4. Wit Promotes Open-Mindedness

Astute witty persons know that humor is the key to rekindle an open mind.[5] They know that deft execution of humor allows them to showcase the universality of life's hardships. It tells the audience—be it comedy club patrons, coworkers, friends or family—that they are not alone. Persons of every stripe and persuasion share the same pain, foibles and concerns. This causes the audience to grow more tolerant and to transcend their own confining bubbles.[5] This in turn reduces social friction that would otherwise persist, unless the witty person's skills dispelled it with prescient jokes and anecdotes.[5]

5. Wit Promotes Critical Thinking

The bulk of contemporary humor pokes fun at persons and circumstances. Consequently, the person who dares to be witty is often in the position of mocking authority figures, exposing ridiculous assumptions and contesting the status quo. Receptive audiences initially guffaw at the witty person's observations. However, the audience's smirks and chuckles soon morph into true critical thinking, once they internalize the substance of the humor and see that the witty person is right. The audience suddenly sees flaws in the order of things and embarks on a quest for improvement.[6]

6. Wit Fuels Creativity

Critical thinking can easily spill over into creativity, if the environment and circumstances are amenable. In fact, humor is so effective in spawning important procedural changes and product improvements that many management circles include humorous icebreaking exercises in their collaborative meetings. Whereas critical thinking unmasks ineptitudes, creativity furnishes novel solutions. The company clown promotes new directions in business culture, workflow and product lines by engaging participants with various antics, promoting commonalities among participants and generally getting their creative juices to flow. Innovations abound in the spheres of work culture and process.[5] Workers, customers and other stakeholders' benefit. Everyone is happy. Comedy is not just for comedy clubs!

7. Wit Tempers Hostility

Being humorous suppresses people's desires to kill or harm other people! This is not hyperbole. In today's stressed out society, persons are continually presented with scenarios that raise the blood pressure and invoke rage. Fortunately, a witty person's innate humor can be the one factor that suppresses people's tendency to be reactionary, defensive and even violent. Witty people can use their skills to diffuse virtually any contentious or dangerous situation by breaking people out of their egocentrism and anger.

3 Essential Elements to Humor and Wit

The dual disciplines of Psychology and Linguistics have shed light on three common factors that underlie most comedic expressions. These theorists argue that all humor is based on "scripts" and deviations from these scripts. Here, a script would be a mental note to self, regarding how mundane events are supposed to unfold.[2] For example; there is nothing inherently humorous about a trip to the doctor or a visit to the bank. In the latter instance, one expects to go into an office, be subjected to dreadful tests and subsequently wait for news on the severity of the findings. While doctors' visits are often tinged with suspense and dread, nothing could be less arousing than a long drive to a bank, a long wait in line, and a staid interaction with a bank teller. Consequently, no one wants to hear about other people's doctors' visits or bank runs, unless of course a witty person tells the tale. A witty person knows that a matter-of-fact rehash of such humdrum experiences is apt to make an audience's eyes glaze over. However, they also know that these same experiences can cause people to convulse in laughter, if properly presented. How do they do it? They employ three essential elements of humor to get the job done.[2]

1. Tension

A lesser man turns a hysterically funny encounter into a thing of boredom by embarking on a rambling setup, blathering on about irrelevant minutia and failing to setup a punch line. The witty person stays clear of these failings and foments immediate tension in his audience. It is clear from the start, that his recent trip to the bank was no ordinary exercise in depositing and withdrawing. From the moment the jokester speaks, the audience is on the edge of its seat anxiously awaiting a payoff. The jokester may lean in with wide eyes. They may speak in a hushed tone as if they are sharing some stupendous secret. Conversely, they may throw up their hands and speak in a manic patter, as if the frustration of all banking frustrations has befallen them. Then, they speak the lines that seal the deal by compelling people to wonder what on Earth has happened: "'What's in your Wallet, they say? More like is that your wallet in your pants, or are you happy to see me? You're never going to believe what I saw in the bank yesterday...."

2. Deviation

The witty person proceeds to tell their story, all the while ensuring that their tale deviates widely from any expectations concerning the tedium of banking. Deviations could include bizarre misunderstandings between customers and tellers, strange individuals waltzing into the lobby, overly aggressive or inept security guards, and the like. The end result is a tale that possesses some similarities to everyday banking yet veers off in on a curiosity-inducing course that causes the audience to listen intently while waiting for a laugh-inducing payload. A prime example of a script deviation is a popular joke in which a chiropractor massages the back of a lawyer while both queue in line for a bank teller. When challenged by the incensed lawyer, the chiropractor exclaims that he felt compelled to practice his art. This prompts the lawyer to exclaim –

"I'm a lawyer. Do you see me [screwing] the guy in front of me?[7]

3. Superiority

The tension that the witty person builds up is released once the punch line is delivered and understood by the audience. The incongruity between expectations and outcome is clearly a huge factor in the tension-releasing laughter that ensues. However, a so-called 'superiority' factor is another, integral part of many successful jokes. In the above example, the audience is apt to feel superior to the touchy-feely chiropractor that knows no boundaries and proceeds to grope the

17

man in front of him. Likewise, many people perceive themselves to be more morally pure than the 'shyster' lawyer. It is this sort of superiority that drives laughter in contemporary audiences and has done so since the beginning of time. Witty people know that audiences enjoy jokes that have a 'butt' or targeted person or group.[2] Therefore; the witty person makes light of the butt's shortcomings in a way that amuses without offending or alienating.

Where Does Wit Come From?

Theorists once assumed that wit and appreciation for humor was learned much like reading or arithmetic. Consequently, it was speculated that there would be entire cultures in which persons would have no sense of witticism or humor at all, because the groundwork needed for the development of both traits would not be valued, understood or taught. Surprisingly, as of yet, no such society has been found. In fact, in all known cultures around the world, participants are known to have an aptitude for witticism and an associated appreciation of humor.[8] Even the youngest society members evidence this. Even constituents of all four groupings of non-human primates are known to exhibit humor and wit of some sort.[8] Therefore, the question remains. Where do these aptitudes come from?

Surely the prevalence of rudimentary wit and humor across species of all ages must provide some clue to its origin. It is well known that babies are able to smile within weeks of their births. They start laughing soon afterward, and it is not long before the smallest of children find amusement in simple games like peek-a-boo. While less likely to be known, the non-human primates are much the same. Some emit a kind of laughter, form facial expressions akin to smiles and play a variety of games. Scientists note that at least one species of monkey's finds great pleasure in scaring one another with false alarms only to emit raucous laughter when the ruse is discovered.[9] Apparently, the only difference amongst humans and our closest animal cousins is the depth and breadth of our humor and wit. An animal's humor and wit is tied to its percepts or its immediate experiences of self in the moment. Humans' sense of self is not so shackled to the here and now. Instead, human experience pulls from a wellspring of past memories mixed with more immediate perceptions. Humans have advanced imaginations, and they are able to appreciate abstract concepts such as incongruity or deviation from rational expectations.[5] Consequently, humans are able to identify and react to such deviations with a variety of responses such as curiosity, awe and even humor.[9] Thus, while humor and the ability to be witty is part of the culture of many species, it is only fully developed in our own kind. This lends credibility to the notion that humor is innate to a variety of species and that evolution is the driver behind its increasingly complex manifestations.[8]

Talk of a genetic basis to humor may naturally lead one to believe that there is a humor center hidden away somewhere in the brain, much of the same way that there is a speech center in the brain. However, scientists do not believe this to be the case. To date, no such center has been found.[2] Instead, the capacity to be humorous and to understand humor appears to be spread across multiple neural networks fanning through the frontal and temporal lobes in the cerebral cortex, the so-called "rational brain." This is that portion of the brain that also facilitates speech.[2] Consequently, humor often manifests itself as a kind of wordplay that challenges these interrelated cerebral networks. The story does not end there, however. Humor is not a brain-only phenomenon. It invokes several systems in the body. When humor is experienced, several systems come into play above and beyond the brain. These systems include one's muscular, respiratory, immune, endocrine, and cardiovascular systems and the remaining portions of the central nervous system.[8]

So how does it all work? The wordplay of the witty person stimulates the brain(s) of their audience. This spawns a plethora of activity across the internal systems of all those involved. The audience's heart rate increases. Blood pressure and muscle tension increase with a corresponding surge in circulation. Breathing increases. The body then persists in this state of excitation until the punch line of the joke is delivered and understood. The brain then releases chemicals that promote relaxation, and the body returns to stasis.[8]

What Makes People Witty?

As show earlier, wit is bred right into the genetic fabric of people. Almost everybody born today has the propensity to become a great wit, though many seldom do. Further, this capacity for wit manifests itself in differing forms from one individual to the next. In fact, there are differences in expression of wit specific to families, communities, and entire nations.[8] Nevertheless, the up and coming witty person need only exploit a few techniques and cultivate a few traits to exploit their innate gift.

First and foremost, potential witty people need to cultivate their own sense of humor.[9] One will never attain the status of comedic genius, if they see everything around them cast in a negative light. Surely, there will be all manner of disheartening, disconcerting and downright unpleasant events all throughout one's life. However, the witty person lets life's indignities roll off their back like water off a duck. Further, the witty person often exploits unfortunate circumstances and turns them into source material for humor that others can appreciate, by virtue of having suffered themselves. George Carlin is exceptional in his ability to recast blood-boiling experiences like road rage into fodder for sidesplitting one-liners. For example, Carlin knows that most people have experienced extreme tension and anger due to incompetent drivers. Therefore, Carlin recasts his own bristling experiences into comical observations that others can surely appreciate. In one famous joke, he exclaims –

"Have you ever noticed that anyone driving slower than you is an idiot, and everyone driving faster than you is a [bleep] maniac?"[10]

It is a willingness to laugh at these experiences that fosters a mindset from which wit and humor can arise. Notwithstanding, there are limitations to where one may be humorous and what constitutes appropriate humorous material. Most, if not all persons would deem funerals to be inappropriate venues for merry-making. Persons should not launch into bomb jokes at airports in this current clime. Jokes pertaining to national tragedies or natural disasters may not be welcome for years, if ever. Humorous persons should ply their talents at parties, dinners, and other venues where people expect the atmosphere to be light and humorous. Furthermore, humorous people should generally avoid truly tasteless subject matter.

It is not sufficient for a venue and material to be appropriate. The intended audience must be receptive to the joke itself.[9] While one may not be at an actual funeral, attempts to joke with persons recently bereaved may equally fail. Anxious persons who fear being made fun of or persons from cultures where impromptu joking is offensive may also resist attempts at merriment. Consequently, the witty person needs to ensure that the target audience is amenable to whatever amusement he intends to bestow. Witty persons in advance of any sustained acts of wordplay or physical humor scrutinize subtle clues like perceived state of mind, body language and initial reactions to mild jest. Closed body posture or other stances and expressions signaling disinterest or distress should be noted and should put an immediate end to one's attempt to make merry. However, if the target audience leans in and their eyes widen with expectation, it's time to let loose.

Finally, witty persons must remember that jokes must not be so obvious that the punch line can be interpreted immediately or even anticipated in advance. However, punch lines cannot be so hard to understand that they are virtually inscrutable.[9] Jokes are not foreign films. Persons do not want to go home and ponder them for days.

Case Study #1: Groucho Marx

In every generation, there are individuals who look back on the olden days with great fondness. There is always a niche market for vintage clothes, early cinema and old books, and certain individuals will always long for a perceived golden age. Old comedy buffs are especially likely to muse about the antics of late greats like Lucile Ball, Laurel and Hardy, Buster Keaton and Groucho Marx. However, these comedians should not be lamented as dusty old memories of days gone by. Instead, comedians like Groucho laid the very foundation for what is considered funny today. In fact, Groucho himself has much to teach persons who want to be witty and they are remiss, if they do not study his example.

Why focus on Groucho Marx? Groucho is best known for his Marx Brothers movie franchise. While funny, Groucho's comedic styling was as thick as his grease paint eyebrows and mustache. Groucho and his band excessive use of slapstick, sight gags, and impromptu outbursts of song.

ibes one of the brothers' movies as 'zany' and filled with 'mayhem.'[11] Another article characterizes a brother as 'berserk.'[12] While a great many people can appreciate zany berserkers committing mayhem on the big screen, few envision any positive payoff for exhibiting crazed behavior at office parties, dinner parties or dates. This reality was as evident to Groucho, as it is to anyone else. Consequently, Groucho revealed his comic genius by reworking his witty persona for the venue of television. So great was Groucho's transformation that a scholarly article declares that there are virtually two Groucho Marxs.[13]

Groucho found great success in cinema by playing bizarrely attired con men that womanized and excoriated corrupt persons in authority. However, when the 'Bet Your Life' television opportunity arose,

Groucho rightly surmised that his usual fast-paced shtick, insults and physical humor would not play well on TV. The small screen medium was not an appropriate venue for big screen humor, so Groucho varied his image considerably.[13] Groucho lost the fake facial hair and oversized, black coat. He dispensed with the pratfalls and silly walks and replaced them with well-timed eye rolls. He slowed down his comic patter and changed its overall timbre. He forewent the anti-establishment "attack humor," for which he had been well known, and adopted a more self-deprecating style. While the television show was somewhat scripted, he still made room for ad-libs. He let contestants take the upper hand, and he was careful not to take easy advantage of tongue-tied participants. This is a clear example of Groucho's agility, and it should be used as a model for witty persons.

The take away is clear. Humor appropriate to one arena may not be appropriate for another. Outrageous humor that relies on pranks and personal barbs may succeed on screen, but a more measured and considerate approach need be taken in real life. Likewise, witty persons need not feel the urge to upstage other individuals when the opportunity presents itself. Witty persons should endeavor to make any situation fun for all, and that involves both restraint and inclusion. Witty persons—however adept they are—should also equip themselves with a variety of preconceived scripts, as even the most quick-minded of individuals may come up short while fishing for material with which to entertain. This global and varied approach worked so well for Groucho that his jokes and memories have survived him and continue to endear him to comedy enthusiasts to this day.

Case Study #2: Robin Williams

Robin William's untimely and tragic passing touched a nerve with persons all around the world. Perhaps President Barack Obama said it best when he eulogized Williams as a man with many personas who had a singular and touching effect on his audience's spirits.[14] The roles that Williams has played in contemporary film are so ubiquitous that little need be said about his undeniable wit and humor. However, there is perhaps an unspoken lesson to be learned for those who use Williams as a model, as they grow and progress in their own comedic abilities.

Williams was born in Chicago on July 21st, 1951. Unlike many entertainers, he was not born into show business, and his preternatural ability to make people laugh was not evident at an early age. Instead, Williams was characterized as a shy and retiring child.[15] In fact, quite late in childhood, high school classmates still voted him "Least Likely to Succeed."[15]

Fortunately, Williams' burgeoning interest in comedy and acting was not deterred. Prior to High School, Williams had already honed his impersonation skills by mimicking an aunt's southern accent.[15] Later, exposure to Kubrick's film *Dr. Strangelove* spawned in Williams a desire to become an actor, and he formally pursued this avenue through his high school drama department.[15] Ultimately, Williams would attain a coveted slot at Juilliard, an elite school for the performing arts.[15]

Williams' entry into Juilliard did not put him on a clear-cut path to success. While his instructors truly enjoyed his impersonations, they felt that his manic style and improvisational flair were incompatible with stage and screen acting. Consequently, instructors urged Williams to pursue a career in stand-up comedy, and he obliged.[15] Williams's comedy club routines are lauded today. However, success was not immediate. Williams worked a number of clubs and then acquired a brief spot on Richard Pryor's NBC television show.[15] While these early opportunities were short-lived, they paved the way for Williams to play the titular role of Mork from Ork.[15] From here, Williams went on to a more storied career as a seasoned stand-up comedian. His entrée into film was also launched starting with perceived flops like *Popeye* and *Garp*.[15] Fortunately, Williams finally ascended to the status of acclaimed and bona fide actor with the release of *Good Morning, Vietnam*.[15]

Robin Williams will be forever remembered as Aladdin's genie sidekick, Peter Pan, Mrs. Doubtfire and a variety of other heart-warming characters. Some will know him as an exceedingly raunchy comedian, and others will know him as the deranged and seemingly dangerous man who developed family photos in *One Hour Photo*. Whatever the case may be, the depth and breadth of Williams's acting and comedic abilities took him far in life. As mentioned before success was not immediate. Williams had to first overcome his shy nature to facilitate pursuit of his dream. When his natural abilities proved incongruous with his initial desire to work in film, he branched out to venues were patrons were more apt to appreciate his high-strung improvisation. Then and only then did he use his comedic laurels to secure bigger and better roles in films. Though there were flops along the way, Williams stayed the course and became the versatile entertainer that we know today. Anyone looking to be witty should realize that even the late, great Robin Williams struggled mightily in his career, but he accepted no roadblocks. He forged ahead and realized a dream. Hence, witty persons must strive to cultivate the same fortitude, tenacity and alacrity as they seek their own public or personal success in the arena of wittiness.

9 Actionable Steps to Becoming More Witty

There are nine basic steps that anyone can employ to become wittier. Below they appear, in no particular order –

1. Appreciate the Humorous Potential of Persons and Situations

Virtually any situation can be made humorous with a few notable exceptions (e.g., national tragedies). Even soul sucking, life wasting trips to the Department of Motor Vehicles or DMV can turn into high comedy adventure, if you know how to manage it. Unimaginative persons are apt to hem and haw in line, thus adding to the misery. However, you—as a developing witty person—should endeavor to entertain fellow sufferers with your wordplay. The DMV may not appear to be ripe fodder for any kind of fun. However, there is a wealth of material for the astute mind. Insane state laws are a prime example. Poking fun at types of drivers you hate should win approval. Everyone knows "those drivers." Comic musing over all those other things you could be doing will surely strike an immediate chord with others thinking the same.

2. Match Your Humor to the Situation

If you are going to be in line for hours, no one will want to hear rapid-fire puns. That would be punishment, pun intended! Therefore, it is prudent to switch up your humor style for the demands of the occasion. A DMV trip would be a fine time to break out into a tall tale that has some sort of bearing on the situation. In the context of a DMV, you could easily launch into a "based on a true story" account of a cross-country road trip in a jalopy with dubious insurance and expired plates. Such a saga is apt to grow increasingly outlandish, as you recount pursuits by various local police with varying attitudes and regional characteristics. Everyone—including DMV staff—will likely hang on your every word, as they await the outcome of your high-stakes adventure.

3. Employ Comedic Tone & Facial Expressions

Don't drone on about the nuisance that is small town cops. Don't sideline off into the minutia of big cities or stick on the tedious aspects of travel through flatter, deforested and unpopulated states. Instead, employ pacing and expressions that would make Groucho or Robin proud. Pair harried hand gestures and rapid-fire speech to recount weaving through NYC side streets where hardline cops abound. Obviously, you are on the run! Then, switch to a slowed speech pattern and somnolent gestures to underscore the tedium of driving through beautiful, but boring Midwest farmland. Be sure to stop abruptly, look around and speak in a hushed manner, while you narrate that part about the cop you saw lurking behind the suspiciously placed billboard. Did that cop spy you and your broken headlight? People will be waiting to find out.

4. Make Use of Impersonations

If you are capable, throw in some comical impersonations. Obviously, you don't want to engage in a rude mockery of persons from different parts of the country. However, if your travels took you through Maine, add a drawn out "Ayup," as you reenact the apprehending officer's speech. If you found yourself stopped in Canada, add a loaded "Ey?" to the end of statements that you recount the officer saying. You may also want to mimic regional changes in speech rate or differences in gesture or phrases. It's time to channel that languid Midwesterner who told you that the state line was "aways over there, around the bend and up yonder."

5. Switch Up Your Routine

More than one single story will be needed to while away your time at the DMV. Unless the breadth and depth of your college vacation rivals *War and Peace*, you will need to switch things up. Suppose number 435A is called in the middle of your tale. An older gentleman may then be observed toddling toward a clerk only to see a young woman dart in front of him. You see him look at his number, scowl, flap his arms and sit back down. Surmise that this poor, old soul must have 485B! Humorously, jest about the intensely irritable thoughts going through this man's mind. Blame the DMV on his aged appearance.

6. Encourage Others

Your attempts at humor may not be the only attempts at humor. If others chime in, engage in a back and forth repartee with the other individual. If you and your line mate are paying off double-parking tickets, make light of yourselves as heinous criminals. Baulk about how you will be set back financially do to the overwhelming fees. Make fun of the circumstances that caused you to double-park in the first place.

7. Make Use of Wordplay

Be sure to employ wordplay where possible. Wordplay is hard if you don't feel sufficiently quick-minded and verbally flexible enough to hold-forth with adept practitioners. However, sparing use of puns suffice. Plays on state names, unusual regional words and words that are fraught with innuendos can add to the color of your humor.

8. Mentally Prepare for Hecklers

Remember that certain persons will want to one-up you for a variety of reasons. Be prepared. If you sense a contentious battle of wits, attempt to anticipate where the direction is going, and have one-liners and comebacks at your disposal. Situations like a DMV visit are very trying, and your wit may provoke the ire of the one Midwesterner who has come to acquire temporary plates. If in doubt, try to deflect. Explain to the Midwesterner that in your parts, people "bang a U-ee" and pull other, strangely worded driving maneuvers. Therefore, you just find it comical that the Midwest has its own regional flair. Then, ask him what he finds unusual and funny about the new environment in which he finds himself.

9. Keep it Friendly

Remember that humor should create a pleasant environment. Regardless of your own propensities, if you want to succeed in a social environment, gage your audience's reactions and ensure that you are raising the morale around you and not killing it. The mom with the four tots may not want to hear your raunchy sex jokes. A Latino person may not care to hear you butcher a Spanish dialect, as you reminisce about your seedy side excursion into Tijuana. Elderly persons may not want to hear you state your opinions about older drivers on the road, despite how funny they may otherwise be. Employ common sense and courtesy in mixed environments, and you will be on track to mastering witticism.

How to Think Outside the Box to Become More Witty

Reliance on canned jokes can only take witty persons so far in their quest to entertain. Unless one is a toastmaster or professional comedian, one is likely to know only a handful of jokes by rote. Applying these jokes to diverse situations can be a challenge. The demands on memory are intense, and the ability to retailor jokes on the fly is not shared by all. Consequently, witty persons run the risk of flubbing comedic interchanges, if they are not on point with their joke making. To avoid potential disasters, witty persons need to think outside the box to ensure that every foray into wit is a successful one.

As stated before, there are entire models of humor and joke making of which one can apprise one's self, as one learns the craft of wittiness. However, these models can be time consuming and also difficult to employ in novel situations. Therefore, one should start with easier models to increase and advance one's wit capabilities. One easy way to proceed is to be overly literal. By way of example, consider the greeting "What's up?" The correct response would likely be "Not much. And you?" However, an overly literal person would look up and scan the skies for some unknown object. This is by no means side splitting, but it conveys the idea. A better example might be:

Bystander: So Pat Robertson, Satan, and LeVar Burton walk into a bar…

Witty Person: Really???!

Here, a bystander has initiated some joke. However, the witty person intercepts it with an incredulous reply, which adds a whole new angle to the interchange. Again, this is not apt to slay persons with laughter, but it illustrates the point that humor may be injected in the simplest and most unexpected ways.

Other means of infusing humor into a conversation involve the use of euphemisms, withholding of euphemisms or underscoring the inanity of euphemisms.[16] These methodologies involve a slight degree of mental gymnastics, but today's PC and jargon-laden speech provides ample ammunition for anyone looking to incorporate this brand of humor into their repertoire. A prime example of euphemism-driven humor appears in a New Yorker cartoon featuring the tombstone of a 'corporate warrior.' The epitaph reads in part: "Took it to the next level."[17] This very humorous caption is in essence the redefinition of death itself using corporate lingo. On the flip side, withholding euphemisms, when euphemisms are due is also a valid tactic in humor. Consider the following exchange:[16]

Person A: "Well she stood me up. She didn't call. And she didn't apologize afterwards."

Person B: "Sounds like she's a..."

Witty Person: "...@$#&*?".

Here, readers should substitute @$#&* with the most uncharitable word that comes to mind. This is funny, since polite society dictates that its members sugarcoat things where possible, therefore, the person who daringly speaks it 'like it is' gets the laugh. Similarly, calling euphemisms out should garner laughter from persons who are tired of resorting to contorted and benign ambiguities to prevent offense. If a person is stumbling to pitch a blind-date prospect as….well…"under-attractive," call it out for what it is. He's UGLY!

Thinking outside the box entails switching things up. Too much euphemism or literalism is akin to too many puns. It's never a good thing. For other methods of humor, look to the likes of comedians such as George Carlin. Carlin created a whole comedic cottage industry by pointing out misunderstandings in the way common terms are employed. For example --

Healthy does not mean "healthful." Healthy is a condition, healthful is a property. Vegetable aren't healthy, they're dead. No food is healthy. Unless you have an eggplant that's doing push-ups. Push-ups are healthful.[18]

This is wordplay at its finest. It subtly employs scripts pertaining to proper use of grammar, the vegetable and eggplant references are deviations, and superiority is likely to be felt by persons tiring of "crunchy types" who overuse "healthy" as a buzzword. It also showcases how all this can be condensed in the simple exercise of pointing out fallacies in language application. Thus, thinking outside the box need not be viewed as a herculean task accessible only to linguistics and stodgy grammarians. It is a skill accessible to all who want to learn, and the benefits are a quick and easy application of wit in any circumstance.

How to Improve Your Vocabulary to Take Wittiness to the Next Level

Let's face it. Most of today's humor revolves around creative wordplay and witty repartee. Unless you are a seasoned vaudevillian comedian, pratfalls, eye poking and other forms of physical comedy will not achieve anything apart from painful looks or an escort out the door. Therefore, make sure you are "armed" for any potential battle of wits that involves back and forth verbal exchange. The first and best way to prepare is through an increase in your own vocabulary, as words will be your primary weapon of choice.

It is a simple matter to increase your vocabulary. One of the easiest ways to proceed is to read books and other printed literature. Of course, keep your aim in mind. Reading *The Economist* or legal journals will not do you any favors, unless you are in the niche business of roasting businessmen and lawyers. Instead, you should spend your time consuming biographical material on comedians and great comedic works. This will boost your vocabulary whilst providing insight into the way in which the words are skillfully employed to the benefit of the comedian. These books will showcase masterful joke examples and generally make use of words in a humorous and well-crafted fashion.

Read a dictionary. No, seriously…. Dictionaries can be viewed as staid tomes of boredom, or they can be seen as an arsenal in your quest for witticism. A standard issue dictionary is going to list etymologies, literal meanings of words and archaic words. Think of the possibilities! You can employ your new and advanced language skills to delight highbrow audiences at dinner parties, or you can use them to impersonate and take down a pompous butt of your jokes. Puns and jokes pivoting around overly literal use of nouns also become easier to contrive, if you are acutely aware of word definitions. Dictionaries also reveal double entendres and slang usage. Pay special attention to any words that possess both innocuous and explicit meanings, as these words are a gold mine for jokesters. TV commentator Carenza Lewis inadvertently discovered the power of double entendre when she innocently stated that people would "eat beaver" if they could get it.[19]

Here, it is abundantly clear that Ms. Lewis failed to recognize the breadth of meanings attached to the term "beaver." As dictionary.com points out, "beaver" is a crude term for female anatomy.[20] An acute awareness of non-standard usage of common words—like "beaver"—can save persons such as Carenza from embarrassing predicaments. These less common definitions may also be deliberately employed to good end by risqué jokesters. Double entendre is also particularly effective, because it allows witty persons to utilize all manner of jokes in a broader range of environments without courting offense. It allows younger members of an audience to appreciate jokes while sparing them from adult connotations. It also helps witty persons save face, if prudes become horrified at some off-color jest. In this latter event, the witty person simply looks at the prude with a "my, what a dirty mind you have" expression. This deflects animosity, and causes the prudes to reconsider their own interpretation of the jest.

Speaking of slang, be sure to peruse in-print or online urban dictionaries. Urban dictionaries will surely boost your wit vocabulary to the next level, as they are rife with contemporary and humorous takes on words and employ these words in fantastically funny, sample sentences. Dictionaries like this do almost all the work for you!

Similarly, obscene foreign language dictionaries provide instant fodder for jokesters. Books like *Dirty Russian* and *Scheisse! The Real German You Were*

Never Taught in School help one expand one's joking abilities by providing immediate access to profane words that one would never learn otherwise. One must proceed with caution, though. Appropriation of another culture's slang may be offensive or hurtful, when natives perceive outsider use of those words as a means to poke fun. However, use of foreign slang may be rightly used to add realism to one's own stories travel stories. Use of foreign slang may also pique the attention and aid the understanding of a bilingual audience.

Finally, onomatopoeia—an often-underappreciated genre of words—can provide a complement to your witty verbal gymnastics. Not familiar with onomatopoeia? Words that fall into this genre are meant to mimic animal and other sounds that cannot be formally spelled out in plain, English language. "Moo" and "baa" are prime examples. However, witty persons do better to conjure up Chef Emeril or the classic

Batman television series. Bang! Pow! Bam! That's onomatopoeia. Captain Marvel utilized onomatopoeia when uttering the word "Shazaam," and the annoying catchphrase "Ba-Da-Bing" is yet another prime example of how these sound-based, non-sense phrases live on in popular parlance. Put simply, these words cause laughter, because they enable the witty person to give voice to the horrible sound that Dave's pants made when they ripped apart in plain sight of everyone. They likewise allow the audience to cringe along with the mechanic who repeats the litany of ridiculous sounds made by grandma as she reviewed her car's recent troubles. Onomatopoeia is silly, and sometimes silly is called for.

How to Avoid Conversation Lulls with the Help of Wit

Even at the most stirring events, there will be times when a conversation appears to go dead. This can be disconcerting, especially for the person newly endeavoring to become witty. Fortunately, this can be an opportune time to test your skills, as there are a variety of ways to turn a dying conversation into a lively success. You simply need the know-how to do it.

One of the easiest ways to revive a dying conversation is to comment on the awkward nature of the situation itself. Simply acknowledge the situation and liken it to a similarly awkward or embarrassing experience in your own past. Start off a conversation with a line like "I don't know about you, but mandatory company parties are always so painful. This reminds me of the time that Dave from the Planning Department...."

Then, renew the conversation with the sad saga of Dave, the ill-conceived open bar Christmas party and the ensuing company lawsuit.

After exploiting this line of talk, you should look around for other awkward pairings, humorous events or unusual surroundings. Easy targets would be mystery food or unusual décor. Everyone of a certain age should be familiar with George Carlin's "is it meat or cake" routine. If you come across similarly inscrutable foodstuff, tip your hat to George and treat your partner to a rehash of Carlin's memorable skit. If pretentious decor abounds, make light of it. Certain furnishings are called conversation pieces for a reason.

If it becomes clear that your conversation partner approves of your brand of humor, you might migrate talk over to other persons in the milieu. Parents trying to corral unruly children or mismatched couples may be the source of gentle merriment. It is not easy to miss older, married men ogling the bosoms or behinds of younger woman. If you see a woman upbraiding her man for such scurrilous behavior, rework a joke like this into your conversation –

After the party, as the couple was driving home, the woman asks her husband, "Honey, has anyone ever told you how handsome, sexy and irresistible to women you are?" The flattered husband said, "No, dear they haven't." The wife yells, "Then what the heck gave you THAT idea at the party tonight?"[21]

While jokes about others usually elicit smirks or laughter, be cautious. Overdoing people jokes can cause people to peg you as a bully. Therefore, be sure to switch things up with some self-deprecation!

Finally, jokes are great, if you have a wide supply of appropriate material to pull from and a great memory to boot. However, memory gaffes, poor delivery of another's material and even a lack of jokes to fit a context can leave you dead in the water. Therefore, opt to use a more organic approach to the situation. As stated many times, jokes are easy to devise. There are two, possible approaches that may be taken to surmount lulls. If originality is not your thing, come up with a skeleton joke that can be tailored to any conversation. Just remember the basics of the script, the pivotal incongruity and the punch line of the joke. Then, once you master reworking jokes from skeletons, employ methodology number two. This entails recognizing the scripts applicable to the environment in which you find yourself, creating an incongruity of your own, and crafting a unique punch line.

How to Build Confidence in Your Witty Remarks

Since time immemorial, comedians have feared radio silent audiences and hecklers who might gain the upper hand. As some have put it, "Comedians kill 'em when they laugh, but die when they don't."[22] This fear is so pervasive among funny men that entire movies have been written about the subject. The stakes are even higher in this day and age, when a bad or inadvertently offensive joke causes one to become a laughing stock on Facebook or to be excoriated on the world stage. Comedian Daniel Tosh's "rape joke" is one example of a joke gone so horribly wrong that he's alienated virtually everyone on the planet.[23] Given the potential for grave disaster, how can the average joe embark on a path of witticism without letting fear and doubt consume him?

Professionals who have fine-tuned their crafts have their own set of mantras and methods that they use to combat negative self-talk that might cause them to lose their edge.[24] Essentially, they use a wide variety of techniques to steel themselves in advance, thereby creating immunity to the sort of trauma that can ruin the aspirations of budding comedians and lay folk alike. Most of these successful comedians know—as a rule of thumb—that beginners go down in flames, and most have lived the horror themselves.[24] This comes as no surprise to them, and they weather through anxiety and bad experiences. While some newcomers are comforted by this realization, others remain terrified at the prospect. These persons need to further steel themselves by asking themselves, what is the worst that can happen?[24] Would-be humorists fantasize about knocking the audience dead with laughter and reaping in subsequent accolades. However, if a joke or series of jokes fails, the end of the world is not likely to be inevitable. People may yawn or roll their eyes. People may be disappointed by the comedic letdown, and more malevolent audiences may join in heckling. However, this needn't put a stop to one's humorous endeavors. Instead, this should be the start of a life-long learning experience that only sharpens one's wit through trial by fire.[24]

The thick skin that develops in response to hard-learned lessons is an effective buffer against fear of failure. However, what can one do in advance to build confidence in one's wit ability? First, one must know what one fears the most in a comedic situation?[24] Is it hecklers, bored facial expressions, dead silence? Once one knows what one fears, one can plan accordingly. If being upstaged by hecklers is the primary concern, there are myriad resources to combat them. The essence of any approach is to forgo offense or disarmament. Comedians have successfully gained the upper hand in a heckling situation through a number of tactics. Some have actually agreed with the hecklers. Some have turned the tables by proceeding to offer hecklers comedic therapy, and some have even brought hecklers onstage and invited them to tell jokes, while the audience turns on them![25] If boredom is the issue, one need only ensure that jokes don't fall into the categories of stories told over and over again, "you had to be there" stories or jokes that hinge on the same scatological pay off over and over. How many barf and toilet jokes can one feasibly take? Instead, one should employ outside the box thinking to keep his routine fresh. Dead silence is easily countered by roping the target audience in with jokes and other witty exchanges that require that audiences participate.

Once one is adequately prepared for the unpredictable, one need only know that most audiences want to be entertained and will give witty people the benefit of the doubt. It is rare that the audience wants to laugh at funny people rather than with them.

5 Actionable Ways to Improve Wit

Humor is a part of the fabric of human nature, and it is almost universally appreciated. However, humor means different things to different people.[2] As you continually strive to improve your wittiness, take the following, advanced strategies into mind.

1. Be Aware of Gender Variances

Men like sexual humor, slapstick and mean-spirited jokes. Women like self-deprecating humor and funny stories.[2] If you are a man in the company of men, let loose with any manner of jokes. There is no onus upon you to have any shame. However, if you are the only man in the company of women, it is best to keep dumb blonde and off-color jokes to yourself. You may also choose not to include excessive use of innuendos. Women may perceive innuendos to be sexual harassment or a "turn on" that you did not intend. If women are the target audience, it is best to poke fun of your unfortunate hair cut or the ugly, Christmas sweater that your children have bought you. Telling tall tales or humorously recounting some convoluted story is an even better bet. Note further that should any deprecatory or sexual jokes be told, the hearer of the joke is more likely to appreciate it, if the butt of the joke is the opposite gender relative to them. For instance, a dumb blonde joke may go down in a female audience if the dumb blonde turns out to be a 'surfer dude.'

2. Be Aware of Cultural Differences

While all cultures seem to express some appreciation of humor, other cultures' approach to and perception of humor are not as straightforward as our own. Even if one is a guy in the company of all guys, one should not assume that the visiting Arabic student or the Pakistani doctor is eager to let loose in riotous laughter over boob jokes or bathroom humor. Chinese culture is a good case study, if one wants to understand the complex nature of humor in other cultures. China is an ancient culture that centuries of divergent philosophies helped to create. One the one hand, China's Taoist history is crucial for instilling the idea that humor is a virtue. Taoism teaches that the advancement of humorous discourse engenders peace, harmony and intellect.[26] On the flip side, China's Confucian tendencies cast humor in a very different light. Confucianism teaches that expressions of wit show one to be shallow. It takes a very puritanical approach to the subject matter and impresses upon adherents that attempts to be humorous with others. It is an informality that breaches long held protocols on what is and is not appropriate in social interaction.[26] In this world view, the only way to be respectable is to be serious and not to show any signs of humor at all.[27] Consequently, Chinese and similar persons may not feel comfortable expressing humor and may be confused as to how to react in humorous situations. Note similarly that Chinese and other non-native speakers of English may fall victim to statements like "What's up." If one catches a person in this predicament, do not make light of it, as one's wit may be perceived to be an insult.

3. Beware of Humor Phobes

Note that there are many people in all cultures that absolutely dread the idea of humorous interaction, because they fear that people are laughing at them or will laugh at them. This fear of laughter and general humor is called gelatophobia. Those that suffer from this unfortunate condition were often the targets of bullying or of some hugely traumatic event that provoked cruel laughter in others.[28] Such persons often fail to appear lively in humorous environments and are noticeably tense. Employ wit techniques that do not mock any persons at all when in the company of someone with gelatophobia. Instead, tell tall tales or use non-threatening modes of humor such as puns.

4. Employ Advance Humor Strategies

Gender, cultural, psychological and other differences may make one feel that one's attempts to be humorous are likely to result in world disaster. However, this need not be the case. Instead, the master witty person realizes that the same things that can cause ambiguity, misunderstanding and even offense can be employed to humorous end, if done properly. Such a witty person employs the concepts of contrast, merging and accommodation to deliver his humor in a way that is palatable to all.[29] The sole Anglo-American can have a ball in an environment predominated by Hispanic persons, if they properly employ contrast that minimizes the differences between themselves and the audience. The Anglo-American simply needs to make fun of the bland nature of Anglo-American food. The Spanish audience is likely to guffaw in response. Similarly, a straight man can minimize the sense of significant difference between him and a Gay man by

68

humorously ribbing the fact that well-dressed Gay men are the reason his wife came to see him as a slob. Adjustment is simply adjusting the content of the joke for the context of the audience. While some Polish and 'dumb blonde' jokes are legitimately funny, they are likely to be so regardless of the ethnicity or gender of the butt of the joke. While it would be social suicide to tell Polish jokes at the Polish American Society, it may be just fine to tell the same joke with the ethnic element removed. Finally, accommodation would consist of subtle alterations to a joke's delivery to accommodate a diversity of audiences. Young, urban Spanish individuals may find it riotous, if a comedian crisscrosses rapid-fire across English and variety of Spanish dialects. However, the same comedian's jokes may not play well to an older, rural, southern, and more Anglo audience. In this context, one need only preface the joke with a comedic overview of Spanish words and slow the joke's delivery time thereby assuring success.

5. Employ Proper Timing

Timing is everything. However, timing remains poorly understood and little is written on the subject. Still, everybody has some sense of the import and importance of comedic timing. In its most simplistic connotation, it suggests appropriate pacing of speech accompanied by a slight pause before the punch line.[30] Whether or not more is intended or even needed is debatable. However, what is not debatable is that too short a time elapsed between the joke and the punch line results in an audience unaware that the funny part has been reached. Too long of a delay cramps the tension that has built up in anticipation of the punch line.[31] Consequently, one should ensure that one's pacing moves the joke along, and one should employ a brief appropriate pause before the joke's final payoff.

Conclusion

The ability to provoke laughter in other persons has long been held in high esteem. Even philosophers and theologians have broached the subject. Some great thinkers have condemned the propensity to be humorous as a character failing and sign of moral incontinence. However, they appear to be in the minority. Philosophical heavies like Aristotle—a man not remembered for his humor—declare wittiness and humor to be virtues.[9] This invites the question, why does the topic of wit enjoy such sustained appeal and focus? The simplest answer to this question lies in our shared constitution. Humans are programmed to be witty and to appreciate others who are witty. In fact, it would appear that humor is selected for in an evolutionary sense, as the funny guy gets the girl and the funny girl keeps her man.

Upon closer inspection, it seems that the ability to be witty equates to real power. The funny man gets the girl, because his wit identifies him as intellectually gifted. Even more to the point, the witty man's skills enable him to position himself as more superior to alternative mates. It is undeniable that humor has historically had a hostile and aggressive component, and this darker manifestation has caused the targets of that sort of wit to slink away humiliated with no prospect of getting the girl. Fortunately, modern sensibilities have evolved, and humor has evolved with them. Humor no longer need be offensive. It has become more inclusive and revolves around witty wordplay, more so than insults and other barbs. As a result, humor is more apt to foster mutually agreeable outcomes. It provides the cement that holds interpersonal relationships together. It helps diverse groups of people recognize their commonalities. It also drives innovation in corporate settings. Thus it is truly to be valued in our contemporary sphere. This raises a new question, how does one become witty?

The innate capacity for wittiness is our birthright. However, this natural gift needs to be nurtured by anyone one hoping to excel at witticism. Since today's humor has evolved away from derision and the physical antics known as slapstick, anyone wishing to excel at comedy needs to hone their abilities at creative wordplay. The task is not daunting. Persons need only increase their vocabularies and learn the simple mechanics of jokes and other forms of humor. The resulting payoff is well worth it. Great relationships, conversations and workplace successes await the one who dares to be witty.

Final Word/About the Author

I was born and raised in Norwalk, Connecticut. Growing up, I could often be found spending afternoons reading in the local public library about management techniques and leadership styles, along with overall outlooks towards life. It was from spending those afternoons reading about how others have led productive lives that I was inspired to start studying patterns of human behavior and self-improvement. Usually I write works around sports to learn more about influential athletes in the hopes that from my writing, you the reader can walk away inspired to put in an equal if not greater amount of hard work and perseverance to pursue your goals. I wrote this book because I always wondered why and how people became to be known as witty individuals. If there were one key takeaway from this book it would be that being witty is not so much genetic as it is understanding what wit is made up of and how to integrate wit into your daily conversations. If you enjoyed *How to be Witty: The Ultimate Guide to Becoming More Clever, Charming, and Engaging with People* please leave a review! Also, you can read more of my works on *How to be Likeable, Bargain Shopping, Productivity Hacks, Morning Meditation, Becoming a Father,* and *LinkedIn: Life Lessons Learned from the "If I Were 22" Campaign* in the Kindle Store.

Endnotes

[1] Weisfeld, Glenn E., Nicole T. Nowak, Todd Lucas, Carol C. Weisfeld, E. Olcay Imamoğluc, Marina Butovskaya, Jilian Sheng, and Michelle R. Parkhill. "Do Women Seek Humorousness in Men Because It Signals Intelligence? A Cross-Cultural Test." *Humor* 24.4 (2011): 435-62. Web.

[2] Restak, Richard. "Laugher and the Brain." *The American Scholar* (2013). N.p., n.d. Web.

[3] Zajdman, Anat. "Did You Mean to Be So Funny? Well, If You Say So..." *Humor - International Journal of Humor Research* 5.4 (1992): 357-68. Web.

[4] Smith, Melinda, M.A., and Jeanne Segal, Ph.D. "Laughter Is the Best Medicine." *Helpguide.org*. N.p., n.d. Web.

[5] Morreall, John. "Comic Vices and Comic Virtues." *Humor - International Journal of Humor Research* 23.1 (2010): 1-26. Web.

[6] Kerr, Michael. "How Humor Helps with Critical Thinking." *Humor at Work*. N.p., 5 July 2011. Web.

[7] "Lawyers & Legal Jokes." *Twilight Zone*. Prodigits, n.d. Web.

[8] Fry, William F. "The Biology of Humor." *Humor - International Journal of Humor Research* 7.2 (1994): 111-26.

Web.

9 Krichtafovitch, Igor. Humor Theory: Formula of Laughter. Denver: Outskirts, 2006. Print.

10 "George Carlin Quotes." *BrainyQuote.com*. N.p., n.d. Web.

11"Animal Crackers (1930 Film)." *Wikipedia*. Wikimedia Foundation, n.d. Web.

12"Monkey Business (1931 Film)." *Wikipedia*. Wikimedia Foundation, n.d. Web.

13Gehring, Wes D. "Television's Other Groucho." *Humor - International Journal of Humor Research* 5.3 (1992): 267-82. Web.

14"Statement by the President on the Passing of Robin Williams." *The White House*. The White House, 11 Aug. 2014. Web.

15Michael, Shayne. "Robin Williams." *The New Shayne-Michael.COMedy*. N.p., n.d. Web.

16 Michael, Shayne. "Twelve Types of Joke Structure." *The New Shayne-Michael.COMedy*. N.p., July 2003. Web.

17 Chast, Roz. "A Tombstone for a Man Who Brought It to the Next Level, Kicked It up a Not... - New Yorker Cartoon Poster Print by Roz Chast at the Condé Nast Collection." *Condenaststore.com*. Art.com, 28 Jan. 2013. Web.

[18] "If I Were in Charge of the Networks Excerpt from George Carlin's Book, Brain Droppings." *Sense.net*. N.p., n.d. Web.

[19] "Double Entendres." CrazySquirrel.com. N.p., n.d. Web.

[20] "Beaver." *Dictionary.com*. N.p., n.d. Web.

[21] R., Henry. "Joke of the Day." *AskMen.com*. N.p., 1 Apr. 2008. Web.

[22] "Comedians Die When They Don't Kill." *Canada.com*. CanWest MediaWorks Publications Inc., 10 Dec. 2006. Web.

[23] Bassist, Elissa. "Why Daniel Tosh's 'Rape Joke' at the Laugh Factory Wasn't Funny." *The Daily Beast*. Newsweek/Daily Beast, 11 July 2012. Web.

[24] "How Comedians Overcome Fear and Build Confidence." *Positive Comedy Learning Development*. N.p., 20 Feb. 2014. Web.

[25] Patrick, Colin. "11 Ways to Handle a Heckler." *Mental Floss*. N.p., 13 Jan. 2013. Web.

[26] Bond, Michael H., ed. Handbook of Chinese Psychology. Hong Kong: Oxford University Press, 1996. Print.

[27] Liao, Chao Chih. "One Aspect of Taiwanese and American Sense of Humour: Attitudes Toward Pranks." *Journal of Humanities Research 2* (n.d.): 289-324. Web.

[28] Ruch, Willibald. "Fearing Humor? Gelotophobia: The Fear of

Being Laughed at Introduction and Overview." *Humor - International Journal of Humor Research* 22.1-2 (2009): 1-25. Web.

29 Norrick, Neal R. "Interdiscourse Humor: Contrast, Merging, Accommodation." *Humor - International Journal of Humor Research* 20.4 (2007): 389-413. Web.

30 Attardo, Salvatore. "Timing in the Performance of Jokes." *Humor - International Journal of Humor Research* 24.2 (2011): 233-50. Web.

31 Audrieth, Anthony L. "The Art of Using Humor in Public." *Squaresail.com.* N.p., 1998. Web.

Made in the USA
Lexington, KY
15 February 2015